Wisdom Wealth Power: 13 Ways To Turn Your Ideas, Gifts, and Talents Into A Profitable Business!

Marshea Mayfield, 'The Empowered Queen'

info@myprofitsolution.com
601-410-0398

Forward

Marshea is truly unique. Her determination is refreshing, and she's relentless. When Marshea sets a goal, she stops at nothing to achieve it. As one of her Coaches, I'm impressed with her commitment and the amount of work she did to leave her comfort zone.

Few are courageous enough to actually do the things they dream of. When Marshea reached out to me, she was very clear in her intentions. And she was fully self-aware of what was holding her back. Yet, she was vulnerable enough to ask for help. In business, that's a sign of a true professional. The result is a brand that's known for empowerment, and this book gives the reader a glimpse into how Marshea was able to build her brand.

For the woman who is just starting a business, this book lays the foundation and gives direction that will lead to having better efficiencies and better overall success with entering the marketplace. The reader can look forward to her no-nonsense approach and learn from her tell-it-like-it-is style.

Not only has it been a joy to witness Marshea's journey, but it has also been inspiring. She doesn't let excuses get in her way, and she's a reminder that, to obtain wisdom, wealth, and power, you have to do the work.

Tajuana Ross
"The LinkedIn Professor"

Inspiration

This book was inspired by a dear friend and client Felicia Rankins. She's the owner of Salon of Praise. She's my former stylist. She shared her personal struggles and business concerns with me. I offered to help her save her business. May I remind you, I was not a business coach at the time, but I had great experience in the business field. Honestly, I was content with my 9-5 job. My vision was so limited that I could not see myself doing anything more than working my business part time and being happy with my salary and benefits. Felicia trusted me, and we saw her business skyrocket in sales. I'm not sure who was the most excited, her or me.

After seeing her results, I began to think back over my life and question my purpose. In this book, you will learn how to determine if you are operating in your purpose or passion. My reason for existing changed, when I suddenly tapped into my purpose. I saw possibilities and knew that God had entrusted me with a valuable gift. My gift is to help women that had faced adversity or maybe was dealt a bad hand or two. What I know for sure is that these things do cause us to question our abilities, skills, and strengths. However, the strategies and lessons here are proven to help you turn your ideas, gifts, and talents into a profitable business. If I can, so can you!

Dedication

This book is dedicated to two women that labored with me tremendously, and because of them, I'm now the Empowered Queen. My mother Priscilla Dean Avery-Chambers was a woman of character, wisdom, and integrity. She instilled in me the importance of work, respect, and dignity. My mom was hard core and took no mercy on my wimping tears. She said, "You will be a woman one day, and I want you to accomplish all your dreams no matter how challenging life will become." As I became a young lady, my mother expressed how proud she was of me. I am forever grateful. She departed this life October 12, 2006.

My spiritual mom, Pastor Bobbie Ashley Graham, came into my life at the age of 12 as a mother, friend, and leader. Her stern but loving personality equipped me for the leader I am today. I recall as a young child she promoted me to Sunday School teacher at the age of 13, and by the time I was 18, I was booking church trips and handling special projects in the church. Many times I was afraid to fail, and there were times I did fail. I would cry and ask to quit, and she would stand about 5ft tall and say, "Shut up, and suck it up." This is a lesson I will never forget. I witnessed her experience some difficult times, and her faith never wavered. This taught me to trust God wholeheartedly because nothing is impossible for Him. She departed this life on February 04, 2016.

Special Thanks

To my supportive husband, Tyrone Mayfield, who never ceases to amaze me with his love and support. My children, Joseph, Timothy, Timeria, Mikeria, and Makanli, for their understanding during my long hours of work. My sister Kristy Chambers for always being a phone call away. My church family that prays and labor with my family and I. My pastor, Tracy Coleman for her push and belief in me. To all my coaches and mentors that paved the way and shared their greatness with me: Denise Hart, Patrice Washington, Zenovia Andrews, Heather Pickens, Les Brown, Alyson Byrd and Tajuana Ross.

I can never forget some extraordinary people that impacted my journey. Gloria Everett, Cozette White, and Shemekia Murphy. To all my clients, friends, family and father (Lonnie Chambers) thank you!

Table Of Contents

<u>*Wisdom*</u>

Wisdom is the principal thing; therefore get wisdom:
and with all thy getting get understanding.
Proverbs 4:7

Leave Your Hustle Behind

The importance of having an infrastructure in your business has several benefits. One, it identifies you as the expert in your particular industry and others takes you more seriously as you begin to create your brand, build partnerships and network. I would like to expound on that because what I have seen is that so many Entrepreneurs use the word "hustle." Hustle is to move or act energetically and rapidly, to act aggressively, especially in business dealings. Slang for hustle based upon Free Dictionary is,

"To obtain something by deceitful or solicit means; practice theft or swindling. To solicit customers or misrepresent one's ability in order to deceive someone, especially in gambling."

The Infrastructure that I want to share with you is how to lay out your business structure. I also want to give you information on how to choose which structure may be best for you and your small business. I will be very clear and frank, I am not a lawyer and cannot provide legal advice. I am only providing information to support you in your decision making. With that being said, I would advise you to consult a lawyer or CPA.

Sole Proprietorship is the simplest form under which one can operate a business. It's the most user-friendly business formation, and I highly recommend it for a new Entrepreneur. The sole proprietor is the person who owns the business and is personally responsible for debts. You can operate under your personal name or a fictitious name, such as "Profit Solution". This particular business structure is the easiest because of its easy setup. You can create your sole proprietor in under 30 minutes by simply visiting irs.gov.

There are, however, some cons to being a sole proprietor. If for any reason (God forbids) you run into legal problems, you could be sued as the owner. In this case, your personal assets are at stake. The second type of business entity is

Partnership. This kind of activity is organized by forming a partnership with an entity or a living person. I highly recommend you seek guidance from an attorney so that you can establish a legally binding agreement between both parties.

Typically, we should shake hands and agree to go into the business together, which is the legalized bond; however, this is not the way a partnership is formed. I made the biggest mistake by agreeing to go into business with a very close friend with a simple handshake. The company ended horribly, and I lost a friend. The lesson I learned was to always treat the business as a legal entity and have the correct infrastructure in place.

The same steps to creating a partnership are the same as the sole proprietor, but you will choose your partners. Now, what this means is that you and your partner have to make all the decisions equally. Both partners are responsible for what happens in the business, so do not make the mistake of making decisions without your partner playing a role in it.

Personally, I use Limited Liability Company as my legal entity, and I'm sure you've heard of it, many call it LLC. The limited liability company protects you as an Entrepreneur. For example, if someone decides to sue you for something that may or may not have been your intent or your fault, and they win the lawsuit against you, they would not have access to take your personal assets. This includes asset such as land, home, cars, etc.

They can only sue you for what the company owns, ok? So again as a sole proprietor if you are sued, they can sue you for everything that you own. As an LLC you are better protected. Some states do not allow LLC, and to find out if your state allows it, be sure to contact your state Secretary of State. The price for creating an LLC varies from state to state; however, you can usually have this done for less than $1,000.

The next two I will share briefly, but I do not recommend starting up S-corp and C-corp. The Corporation is a body, it is a legal person in the eyes of the law. This means, no one person owns the business. It's managed by board members and officers. The shareholders, those that have ownership, can elect board members and officers to manage the company. This type of corporation is more expensive to set up than any other. You will be required to host annual meetings and pay annual fees and periodic filing with the state.

My desire is to have you seen and respected in the marketplace as an Entrepreneur, not a hustler and to make sure you have the correct infrastructure in place. This does not only affect how you are seen but how you show up! You know how we roll!

Develop Your Business Knowledge

There are three things that you should know before going into business. The reason I feel so compelled to share these three things with you is that I wished someone would have explained this to me.

When I started my very first business, I knew one thing...I was the BOSS. Yes, that's the term I used. I felt proud. I was egoistic. After about 6 months of making no money, then 8 months, 10 months, and by 12 months, we were closed. I quickly lost my ego and pride, along with my $10K investment. There are three top definitions you need to know as an Entrepreneur before starting a business:

1. Chief Executive Officer (CEO) - That will be you, you're the visionary, you're the person making things happen. The person responsible if the business is successful or if the business fails.

2. Chief Financial Officer (CFO) - So many people do not acknowledge this particular role. To be successful, you must adopt the qualities of a CFO. The CFO is responsible for the fiscal (money) part of the business. In most small firms that person will also be you because you need to understand the cash flow of your company. I need you to see your cash flow as a body of water. Water is always moving, never stagnant. You must ensure you're moving in directions that will expand your vision and make room for growth. Some financial resources that I have personally used are Waveapp and QuickBooks.

3. Chief Operating Officer (COO) - Again that person may be you because you are responsible for the day to day operations for your company, that is, how things are operating, customer service, complaints and so on. This is discussed further in later chapters. These

things are of the utmost importance if you are looking to grow your business.

Number One Way To Create Consistent Cash Flow In Your Business

OK, let's get real. We start a business for one, the ultimate reward of FREEDOM. Yes, I know we have unique gifts and talents and would love to make the world a better place, but we have to get PAID.

So let's cut to the chase. The number one way to create consistent cash flow is to identify your ideal clients/customers. I'm sure you've heard this before, but if you do not have people calling to pay you, then you missing something. So please for my sake, forget what you think you know and let's get clear. Is this ok?

For one second think of that one person you just absolutely love to see coming. Even if they have never paid for your services, but they often call on you because you are great at what you do. Ask yourself, what is it that I love about them? Is it their personality, their gratefulness, their trust and confidence in you, their willingness to pay, never complain, often refer people, brag about you, etc.

Once you identify this, you will have identified your ideal customer/client.

Now, this may sound crazy but go with me here. You only need a few of these type people. You no longer have to search and market to the masses because you have your ideal client/customer.

So let's give her a name. Yes, right here. _____ is my ideal client. She is _____, _____, and _____ (characteristics).

When I mastered this, my life changed. I stopped attracting annoying people that I spent more time trying to please and began to create a strategy (which I will share with you) for my customers who were waiting for me. Try it, I promise you will see things turn for the good. I need you to take some time and ask yourself these questions. Let me forewarn you, in the beginning, this will seem so elementary, and you may feel like, what's the point. If you get out of your feelings and really dig deep, you are now on your way to a successful business.

Is my ideal client a male or a female, a child, a boy or a girl? (it can't be everyone).
1. What skills does my idea client not possess?
2. What it is that my ideal client is missing in their life?
3. Where does my ideal client live? Southern, northern, eastern, or western.
4. Is my ideal client/customer married?
5. What type of job does my ideal client have?
6. How much do I desire to make per transaction from my ideal client/customer? Now I'm about to make this make a lot of

sense to you with this question, simple math comes into play.

7. How much money should your ideal client make per year? Let me give you an example here, if you're recruiting a customer and you are hoping to make five thousand dollars a year from this particular client, provided he/she only makes fifteen thousand dollars a year, then something is wrong with that ratio. So this is why it's important to be very precise and clear about the type of person you decide to work with, serve and assist.

8. Where does my ideal client hang out? Libraries, movies, theaters, be specific.

9. What are their pain points? Understand these will help you to resolve a pain in their life, so you must be able to identify what the pain is.

10. List three results you can provide to your ideal client/customers.

Hey, STOP here and answer these questions because the remainder of the book is actionable steps to turn your ideas, gifts, and talents into a profitable business. Skipping parts of the process will only cause you delays, headache, and more frustration.

Making Money While You're Sleeping

Please, understand this, while reading this book. If you are not dependable in your business, then your cash flow will NOT be regular. So let's have a real conversation. How long have you had the thought to be your own boss?

How will a successful business change your life?

I cannot spcak for you, but it gave me complete freedom. Going from a job working 50-70 hours a week to working my own hours was a dream come true. Not to mention the days when I thought my two weeks paid vacation was heaven until I was able to take one every month if I choose. My kids were baffled at the fact that mom can now attend their events, activities, take trips and be home to tuck them in. So, if this is the type of life you desire, you are making the perfect decision by reading this book. I need to push you a little further though, do not just read it, DO THE WORK!

Say this with me:
I'm willing to do ALL that it takes to create consistency in my business.

How to be consistent:

- Remember it takes at least 21 days to develop a habit. Don't stop in a few days thinking "It did not work."
- List all the reasons why a particular task or job will be hard, then come up with solutions for all the problems that may occur.
- Expect to mess up, forgive yourself and keep it moving!
- Show up daily, even at your weakest state.
- Try and focus only on a few things at a time, 2-4 minimum.

"Success does not come from what you occasionally do, it comes from what you do consistently." ~ Marie Forleo

Being consistent in your business will set you up to receive residual revenue. One of my favorite formulas that I personally use and teach to my clients is called the Queen of Cash Flow Formula. The beauty of it is once mastered, you will personally experience the old saying "Making Money While You're Sleeping."

There are six steps to the Queen of Cash Flow Formula:

1. Attract. Offer Something of Value to your Prospect.
2. Engage. Know you have their attention, engage with them.
3. Capture. Know you need a database to collect information.
4. Nurture. Encourage their growth and development.
5. Convert. Persuade them to take action.
6. Measure. Measure your results. What should you do differently?

Consistency makes the job easier. It forms habits and habits lead to success.

Be the Problem Solver

Hey, you're the CEO that means you are the problem solver. Understand that you are the person that solves your ideal clients/customers problems. Your solutions (your expertise) change their lives and add value to your clients/customers problems. Look, they're waiting for you!

I have another formula, and yes, I should call myself Queen of formulas, right. I love formulas because it's like algebra. If you do it the same way every time no matter the numbers, you get the correct answer.

The formula is called PSPS. PSPS equals Problem, Solution, Problem, Solution.

Let me share an analogy. During this analogy, I need you to think of your business and how you can solve problems.

I think I will use me as an example. At the beginning of the year, I decided I wanted to become healthier. I knew it would be a big task because I've always had a problem (problem 1) with my food intake and physical activities. So I instantly found a solution (solution1) and joined the gym. I was thrilled and excited to take action. I went out and purchased matching athletic gear, shoes, gloves, etc. I even told a few friends. Once I got to the gym, I saw the gym equipment, skinny girls running on treadmills and buff men with all their muscles. So you can only imagine the look on my face. I had no clue where to start. The clerk asked, "What's the problem?" I said in shame, "I don't know where to begin" (problem 2). He then recommended a personal trainer (solution 2) who helped me with my problem.

Did you see how they made two sales off one person by continuing to provide a solution to the problem? This is a strategy you must use. This will eliminate the need of always recruiting new clients/customers. Keep your current customers happy and always be their go to person to have their problems solved.

Being a self-confident problem solver is essential to your success. Much of that confidence comes from having a good process to use when approaching a problem.

<u>Wealth</u>

Some people consider family and having many close friends the biggest measure of wealth. Wealth is having good health and being of a sound mind. Spiritual enlightenment is a form of wealth. Wisdom and knowledge are wealth. Intellectual capital is wealth.
Whatever has value for you is a part of your treasure of wealth.
Wealth is having our basic needs met with an abundance of resources in reserve.

Wealth provides a safety net of protection against a decline in one's living standard in case of an unforeseen loss of income or other emergency.
~ Author Unknown

C.L.A.R.I.T.Y Equals Cash

Steve Maraboli — "It's a lack of clarity that creates chaos and frustration, those emotions are poison to any living goal."

One of the most important things in being an Entrepreneur is to be knowledgeable and confident in who you are as a person. This type of confidence comes from being clear about your goals. I desire to help you get clear about your mission, your purpose, and your goals so that you obtain a successful business and create the life that you want. The ability to be easily understood is what you want for your clients, your teammates, vendors, and everyone involved in operating your business.

You must first be clear so you can convey your message and expectations of others. Have you ever given instructions to someone and they made a mess of what you so unmistakably explained? I know this is very frustrating. Two things likely took place: You did not adequately explain it or express your desired expectations or the person simply did not do it correctly. Well, it's easier for us to say they did not do it correctly, but often times it is our lack of proper instruction. Try being very clear with your instructions and relaying it in a way that the listener will have clarity of your desires.

Let's break down C.L.A.R.I.T.Y:
C- Be clear about your desires
L- Limited in a set of distinct benchmarks
A- Attainable goals that are admirable
R- Relevant to your circumstances.
I- Inspiring because this clearly reflects your passion
T- Is trackable and manageable
Y- You become in alignment with your values

"A goal without clarity is only a dream" ~ Unknown Author

You have been dreaming for far too long, it's time to become clear about who you are, who you are made to serve, and how to go about serving your ideal clients.

Purpose vs. Passion

Are you operating in your purpose or your passion? And the question becomes, what is the difference between your purpose and your passion. To help you understand this, I want to share my story. I had worked in the financial industry for several years, and it was normal to be interested in numbers. As a financial advisor and professional tax preparer, I helped families to make financial decisions. I invested years of study, research and over $50,000 in education to obtain the required knowledge in the financial industry. I was passionate about my career.

As I began to become interested in working with business coaches, I was asked these questions, "What are you really good at? What is one thing you do really well? What is that thing people often come to you for?" Of course, my answer was financial support or advice. So my coach suggested that I should be a financial coach, and because I am passionate about it, I agreed. In one year, I began building a brand, creating products, and recruiting clients.

It was going well, but I was not fulfilled. Something was missing. I started getting frustrated with the type of people I was attracting. These people wanted results, but they were not willing to work for their financial freedom. I began to analyze, and question myself. Is this what I desired to do for the rest of my life? It was at that moment when I realized that's not my purpose.

Your passion is something that you are good at doing. It is what you have the necessary skills and qualifications to do it. It is what you would do, even in your sleep. Chances are you're doing them now. You will operate in your purpose even if you're not compensated for it. Today is a great day to start working in your purpose.

Think back to that one thing that has been a part of your life since you can remember. Maybe it's speaking in public, teaching, dressing your dolls, singing, seamstress, decorating, or even making others laugh.

What is your purpose? May you start to experience clarity.

Know the way, show the way and go the way!

Your leadership skills are one of the most valuable assets or attributes that you can have as an Entrepreneur. Unfortunately, we were not born with this trait.

OK, first of all, you must understand what a leader is?

A leader is one who knows the way, they go the way, and show the way to get there. If your actions inspire you to dream more, learn more and do more and become more, then you are a definitely a leader.

Four things you must adapt to be a great leader:

1. Listening skills. It means not interrupting when someone is speaking. Allow them to share before you respond.

2. You must be an excellent communicator, and there are two forms of communication I want to discuss here: Verbal and Written communication. Verbal communication is the use of words in delivering the intended message. Remember to remain calm and focused. Be polite and following some basic rules of treating others the way you desire to be treated.
Written communication includes traditional pen and paper letters and documents, typed electronic documents, e-mails, text chats, SMS and anything else conveyed through writing. Be cautious because your messages can also communicate thoughts and feelings on their own.

3. Be a great decision maker, yes it's critical! This means removing your feelings and emotions and making decisions that are in the best interest of the company's growth. You are the C.E.O. Therefore, you are the person responsible.

4. The delegation, this was the hardest for me. I am transparent so have a little mercy. I felt as though no one could do the job as well as me. I wanted to see and be a part of every aspect of my business. Knowing, I had no experience in graphic design, I tried to do my own (that was a mess). I made all calls, sent out all letters, approved every invoice, paid every bill, made every social media post. You get the picture, right? I spent so much time working on the business until my competitors were running circles around me. See, they were smart. They hired help and actually let the people do their jobs. Now I delegate, I built a trusted team, and now I allow them to operate in their gifts and me in mine. Actually, the lady who proofed my book is my personal assistant. She owns her very own Proofreading company called Perfect Proofing. I wrote the book and sent my draft to her, and the rest is history. Check her out at www.perfectproofingllc.com.

Change Your Circumstances

Do you understand that you are the only person that can change your circumstances? As a young woman growing up in a small town in Mississippi, I had all odds stacked up against me. For one, being raised in a single family home, mother depended upon government living assistance, and my father was not really active. My mom did a fantastic job raising and protecting me the best way she knew how, but unfortunately, I was a victim of rape and molestation.

I blocked this from my conscious mind in hopes that it would go away, but the older I got, the more it surfaced. One day while speaking to an audience, I decided to share my story, and the room was filled with tears. Afterward, women came and shared their story and thanked me for being so transparent. They did not see my struggles, hurt or shame. They saw

a brave woman that had empowered her circumstances.

I was told that I would never finish high
school, get a job and settle down. Those were
the odds against me, but I knew I was the only
person that could make my circumstances different. I tapped into that power that was deep
within me; it took a lot of sleepless nights; it
took a lot of failures; it took a lot of being
talked about. No one understood me, but the
power that I had to change my circumstances,
is what created the woman that you see today.
So when you realize who you are as a person,
take on that power and that ability to change
the outcome of your life. You may be thinking,
why was it important for me to walk in my
ability. For me, it was so that I could create a
better life for my children, and so that the odds
would not be against them. When I embraced
it, I was in the process that became the journey
that changed my life.

**Things change in life, so remember you
own the key to a brighter future in your life.**

POWER

"For nothing will be impossible with God."
Luke 1:37

Winners vs. Whiners

You must have a winning mindset, no matter what obstacle, you face because you will face challenges in your business. You must have the mentality of a winner, now I want you to understand this. There is a difference between a winner and a whiner. I know you can relate to your younger sibling, cousin or playmate that was always whining about things going on in life. Maybe that person was you.

Did you want to be around them? I will be quick to answer, "NO." I just hate when people always expect the worst. You ask them how their day was and they find all the negative things that took place.

So Entrepreneurs, as a winner, there are five things that we must have:

- Self-Confidence, believe in yourself, product, ideas and your services.
- Seek solutions to the problem, do not elaborate on the problem, remember guys, you're the problem solver.
- Be committed to success. Being committed means sleepless nights, sacrifices, going without the luxury and being diligent in reaching your goals and your dreams.
- Patience, as a winner you will develop this trait called patience. We have to learn how to wait on things.
- Set realistic expectations. I know we all have dreams, and some of our dreams are not realistic, so to be a winner in your business be real with yourself. Push yourself but for heaven's sake, do not have a goal to make $100K in 6 months, and you have never made $1k, I'm just saying (in my Wendy Williams' voice).

This part is quite simple: whiners have no confidence, they consistently make complaints, never satisfied with what they are creating, often blame other people for what went wrong in their business, and whiners never face their problems. Whiners are not committed, one day they are here, the next day they're gone.

Use What You Have

Earlier I talked about being clear, and defining your purpose now it's time to own your power. I could go on and discuss ways to write a business plan, how to apply for grants and loans, but it's not the time. Before any bank or lender even considers lending you money, you must prove and justify your business success. So if you scanned through the book only looking for stuff that makes you feel like a BOSS, then I advise you read this book over again so that you can prove to the bankers that you are capable of producing a profit by executing all these simple, but proven strategies in this book.

I'm not a fool, I know it takes money to make money, but check this out. When I started my first company, I had $10K and a business plan, but I lost it all! My second business, I had my kids' computer, a desk from my home office and my passion. Nope, I did not have any money to invest; I had just lost ten grand 8 months prior. I did have three little mouths to feed and a dream to work for myself.

I used my resources, and next year will make it my 10th year anniversary in business. We now service clients across the globe. If you make excuses such as I need more money, need more education, have to do a little more research, never seen this done before, or I have no one to support me, then I say, "get over yourself." Capitalize on your strengths and on the things that you have access to.

Really quick, think of all the resources that you have. List them out here (think of public places to help you like a library, post office, friends, and family).

Power Behind Your Voice

I have said it before, but I really need you to take the time to really do each of the above strategies. In the next chapter, I will share stories and testimonies from clients that are no different from you. They had suppressed their talents and gifts for too long. Today each of them followed the exact steps here, and they are NOW successful Entrepreneurs.

May I ask you a question? How do you use your voice to be seen and heard If your brand is new? No worries I will tell you, but if you have been in the game for a while let's restrain ourselves. Every conversation about your business should be treated as a possible partnership or client recruit. To do this, you have less than 60 seconds to capture their attention.

When you master your Elevator Pitch, you will no longer be caught off guard when someone asks you to "tell us what you do" or "introduce" yourself.

Having a power statement, just one sentence that gets immediately to the core of how you serve the world is essential. An effective statement covers all the key components of the service your provide in one sentence! Here's the formula:

I help [who] do [problem you solve] so that [outcome, transformation or result]
I work with [who] who struggle with [problem they have] so that they can [outcome or result]
I help _____ do
_____ so that

_____.

Example: I help women turn their ideas and gifts into a profitable business, so they can design their dream life.

Don't Take It from Me

Hello, my name is Cindy Miller aka "Comedian Granny" I knew since I was a child that I was destined to be an Entrepreneur! My family owned businesses throughout my childhood. The Lord knew my heart, and divine connections began to take place. That's when I met Coach Marshea Mayfield. I signed up to take a Bootcamp Course and my life completely changed! I had about (7) business ideas; my first assignment was to put the businesses I wanted to start in order. The very next session I had clarity of my business "Comedy" to help my clients Loosen up and Laugh 😃 please note this was not one of my business ideas! The rest is history! The Lord has Blessed me to grace many stages including The Laugh Out Loud Comedy Show, Him Them & Me Comedy Tour & Slidell Little Theatre- A Lesson Before Dying, playing the role of "Miss

Emma" in which I was honored with the Ginny Award for Best Supporting Actress in 2016. Marshea told me something that I will Never Forget. "Sometimes you have to go for it even if you are Scared" and that's exactly what I did when The Lord blessed me to Co-Author my first book! I went from Hobby to having a Successful Business! To God Be the Glory!
Humbled & Grateful,
Cindy Miller, CEO
Book Granny Today
601-381-0648

—

My name is Shantissa Glenn, I am the CEO of Kidz B Kidz Daycare. I always wanted to start my own business but was afraid. I was not only afraid, but I was also scorned and felt like I wasn't't worthy. I grew up in the projects, I was molested at a young age, and I went through a divorce. Through all this, how was I going to start a business with 7 kids of my own, but God! For 10 years, I procrastinated about starting my own business. I thought I had to have a lot of money to get started. In reality, I didn't't. One day God sent Marshea Mayfield to talk to me, and she asked why haven't I moved forward with my dream and vision He gave me. After our conversation and me starting in her program, things took off. Once I made the step in moving forward, God began to open doors for me. Yes, I was scared with no money, but God did just what has He said, and He used Marshea to lead me. I am now going into my second year of business looking forward to much more blessings from God. I'm still learning as I go.

Shantissa Glenn
601-498-9911

—

I am blessed to have been sent to Marshea for a conversation! I am the CEO and owner of Perfect Proofing, LLC. I have been doing proofreading and editing for years, but it was something that I did because people would need me to do it. I was referred to Marshea to discuss a "business opportunity." I prayed about it and talked to God several times to get clarification as to whether I should do this. After many discussions, I reached out to her. However, this was not my first time reaching out to Marshea, but this time was different. I was leading myself and did not get the okay I needed from

God. Needless to say, we did not connect at all! Oh, but after I had prayed about it the second time, I was sent my vessel, Marshea Mayfield.

I talked to her and complained and found excuses as to why this "type" of business would not work. When I finished complaining and finding excuses, she said: "Are you ready to start your business now?" That was the beginning, and we are still on this ride. I complain, she listens and guides me to continue to be great within my business. She assisted in turning my gifts and skills into a successful business! Last, but not least, Marshea has guided me to become a serial Entrepreneur.

Anita Daniels,
CEO and Owner of Perfect Proofing, LLC
www.perfectproofingllc.com
512-965-4346

—

Hi I am Mary Powe, Fitness Diva and I am the CEO of Get IT Done Fitness with Mary. I have been in business for 3 years. Marshea came into my life as a new friend, just hanging out doing exercise and keeping each other company.

Once our workout became routine, and all my friends were seeing results and wanting more, Marshea looked at how I was helping others do the impossible (lose weight). She gave me the proper tools to do what I love to do, helping others, and branch off into a business.

Without her guidance and support, I wouldn't have known that I could get paid for helping others live a fully healthy lifestyle inside and out.
Mary Powe, CEO
601-410-1536

———

Hi my name is Chiquita Brown, and I am CEO of Nspired Boutique. I was on an emotional roller coaster in my business. I knew where I was trying to get but just couldn't seem to find my way. Up one day, all the way down the next! I got so tired, and right before throwing in the towel, I said, "Lord You have to show me what to do." Y'all the next day I found myself sitting in Marshea's office telling her my story.

This lady kept right on working while listening to me and at the end of my pity party, she looked me in my eyes and said to dry up those tears. I think you're ready. She sat down with me, put together a plan and it has been phenomenal.

What I love the most is she doesn't just get your money and leave you when she gives her formula, but she follows you and builds a relationship with you to make sure the results are there.

More than anything, I love that she had an anointing on her life that helps her to assist you and you can see she lives what she speaks! Through the aid of Coach Mayfield, I am excited to be looking to birth out many more Nspired Boutiques. I'm pregnant now awaiting the birth of twins! To be continued....

Chiquita, CEO
Call today and let us dress you!
601-498-9516

My name is Tina Rash. I have been coached/trained/mentored by the Result Driven Coach Marsha Mayfield and before she began helping me, I prayed and asked Jehovah to help me in my business by showing me HOW to work with others. He led me to Marshea.

She taught me how to build relationships, how to be a good listener, how to believe in myself and my products. Whenever I dragged my feet, she encouraged me and told me to listen to the Holy Spirit and be led by Him.

I know God placed Marshea in my life at a time when I had a lot of doubts and low confidence. Though she will NEVER take credit, she cares for all her clients as friends FIRST, teaching us to be independent while we have faith and trust in God.

I know that my business flourished because of her leadership. Marshea continues to be a serial Entrepreneur helping those that genuinely WANT to help themselves.

Tina Rash

To Your Success

Marshea Mayfield

**For more info email:
info@myprofitsolution.com**

**For Bulk Orders or
speaking engagements,
call: 512-965-4346**

www.ingramcontent.com/pod-product-compliance
Lightning Source LLC
Chambersburg PA
CBHW071240220526
45468CB00002B/933